Senior Art Editor Anna Formanek
Project Editor Lara Hutcheson
Managing Editor Tori Kosara
Managing Art Editor Jo Connor
Designer Emma Wicks
Production Editor Siu Yin Chan
Senior Production Controller Lloyd Robe
Publisher Paula Regan
Art Director Charlotte Coulais
Managing Director Mark Searle

Written by Julia March
Designed for DK by Thelma-Jane Rob
Reading Consultant Barbara Marinak

DK would like to thank Hank Woon, Alyssa Tuffey, and the rest of the team at The Pokémon Company International. Thanks also to Lori Hand for proofreading.

First American Edition, 2025
Published in the United States by DK Publishing, a division of Penguin Random House LLC
1745 Broadway, 20th Floor, New York, NY 10019
25 26 27 28 29 10 9 8 7 6 5 4 3 2 1
001-344852-July/2025

A catalog record for this book
is available from the Library of Congress.
ISBN 978-0-5939-6580-1 (Paperback)
ISBN 978-0-5939-6581-8 (Hardcover)

DK books are available at special discounts when purchased
in bulk for sales promotions, premiums, fund-raising, or educational use.
For details, contact: DK Publishing Special Markets,
1745 Broadway, 20th Floor, New York, NY 10019
SpecialSales@dk.com

Printed and bound in China

www.dk.com
www.pokemon.com

Pokémon™

Sweet Surprise

Julia March

DK

Contents

Sound it out

Try saying these Pokémon names out loud.

Alomomola
[uh-LOH-muh-MOH-luh]

Floette
[Floh-ET]

Alcremie
[AL-kruh-mee]

Togepi
[TOE-ghep-pee]

Growlithe
[GROWL-lith]

Pansage
[PAN-sayj]

Full of surprises

Pokémon are all very different.

Drampa

Drampa can stir up a sudden storm.

But they are all full of surprises!

Igglybuff

Sometimes Igglybuff can't stop bouncing.

Healing Pokémon

Did you know that some Pokémon can heal others?

Alomomola

Golden eyes

Handlike fins for hugging

Heart-shaped body

This Pokémon can give a healing hug!

To the rescue

Pokémon love to help save the day.

Floatzel

Two tails

Floatzel rescue people who need help at sea.

Floette

Floette help limp flowers. They make them healthy.

Tasty treats

Some Pokémon might give you a tasty surprise. A dessert made with Alcremie's sweet cream is very tasty.

Alcremie

Miltank

Miltank produce milk. Their milk changes flavor with the seasons.

Sweet sounds

This Pokémon likes to sing among the clouds.

Short beak

Altaria

Fluffy feathers

They wrap friends in their wings. Then they start to sweetly hum!

Happy-go-lucky

Find one of these Pokémon. It could bring you luck!

Togepi

Be kind to a Togepi and it will share its good luck.

Togetic can fill you with happiness.

Togetic

Togekiss

Look out
for Togekiss.
They bring blessings.

Loyal friends

Even fierce Pokémon can be loyal friends.

Growlithe

Growlithe are brave Pokémon. They like to defend their friends. They will bark and bite.

Sharp claws

Thick mane

Stripes

Cheerful dancers

Watch a Pokémon dance. It will change your mood.

Brionne

Brionne's dance makes people happy.

Sylveon

Sylveon's dance is very calming.

Hitch a ride

Come aboard!
These Pokémon are your
travel buddies.

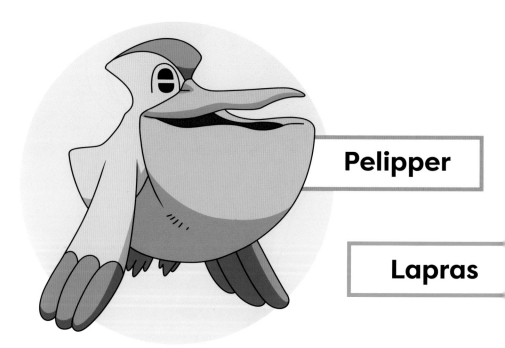

Pelipper

Lapras

Small Pokémon
can hitch a ride
in a Pelipper's
big beak.

Small horn

Lapras love to carry people across the sea. If they are happy they will sing to you, too.

Hard shell

Top teamwork

This pair of Pokémon like to swim together.

Mantyke

Wide, flat fins

Remoraid

Dorsal fin

They help each
other avoid attacks.
They also share
their food.
What a great team!

Gifts to share

Lots of Pokémon are happy to share their gifts.

Pachirisu

Pachirisu share electricity by rubbing their cheek pouches together.

Pansage are kind.
They share berries with
their friends.

Pansage

Leaf

Kind and caring

These kind Pokémon carry a surprise!

Happiny

Happiny might offer their friends the white rock in their pouch.

Chansey's egg can help heal injured Pokémon.

Chansey

Blissey

A bite of Blissey's egg has the power to make you smile.

Glossary

Blessings
Well-wishes, or a special gift or favor.

Limp
Soft and weak, with no strength.

Loyal
Devoted and faithful to someone or something.

Produce
To create or to make happen.

Index

Quiz

Ready to find out how much you learned? Read the questions and then check your answers with an adult.

1. Can Drampa stir up a storm?

2. Which Pokémon produces milk?

3. How do Alomomola heal Pokémon?

4. Do Growlithe sometimes bark and bite?

5. What do Lapras do if they are happy?

1. Yes 2. Miltank 3. With a gentle hug 4. Yes 5. Sing